Modern Middle East Nations
AND THEIR STRATEGIC PLACE IN THE WORLD

BAHRAIN

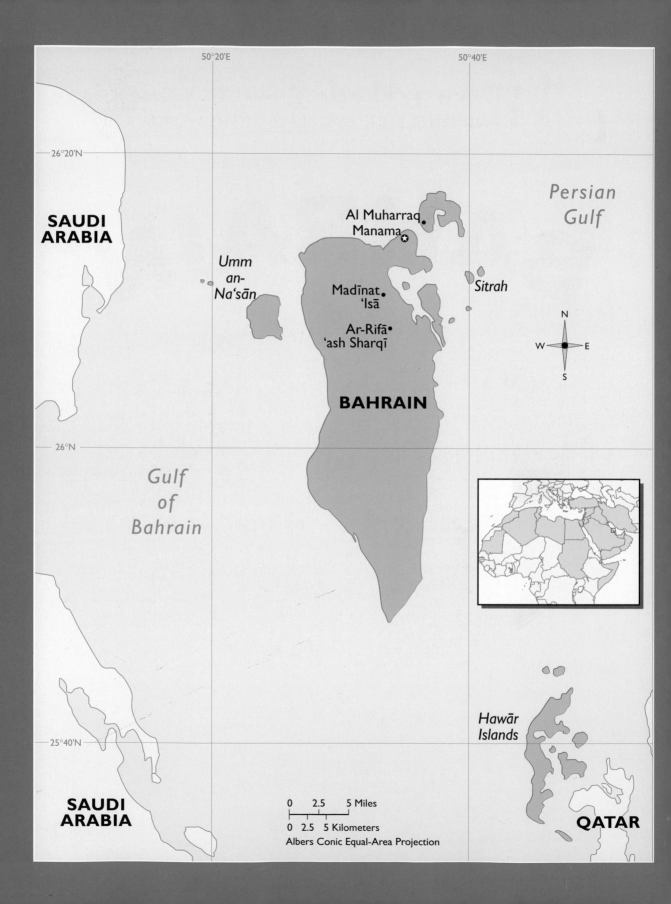

Modern Middle East Nations
AND THEIR STRATEGIC PLACE IN THE WORLD

BAHRAIN

LISA McCOY

MASON CREST PUBLISHERS
PHILADELPHIA

Produced by OTTN Publishing, Stockton, New Jersey

Mason Crest Publishers
370 Reed Road
Broomall, PA 19008
www.masoncrest.com

3 5 7 9 8 6 4 2

Library of Congress Cataloging-in-Publication Data

McCoy, Lisa.
    Bahrain / Lisa McCoy.
        p. cm. — (Modern Middle East nations and their strategic place in the world)
    Summary: Discusses the geography, history, economy, government, religion,
    people, foreign relations, and major cities of Bahrain.
    Includes bibliographical references and index.
        ISBN 1-59084-522-6
    1. Bahrain—Juvenile literature.   [1. Bahrain.]   1.
    Title. II. Series.
    DS247.B2M38 2003 953.65—dc21

                                            2002012996

TABLE OF CONTENTS

Modern Middle East Nations
AND THEIR STRATEGIC PLACE IN THE WORLD

ALGERIA
BAHRAIN
DJIBOUTI
EGYPT
IRAN
IRAQ
ISRAEL
JORDAN
KUWAIT
LEBANON
LIBYA
MAURITANIA
MOROCCO
OMAN
THE PALESTINIANS
QATAR
SAUDI ARABIA
SOMALIA
SUDAN
SYRIA
TUNISIA
TURKEY
UNITED ARAB EMIRATES
YEMEN
THE MIDDLE EAST: FACTS AND FIGURES

Dr. Harvey Sicherman, president and director of the Foreign Policy Research Institute, is the author of such books as *America the Vulnerable: Our Military Problems and How to Fix Them* (2002) and *Palestinian Autonomy, Self-Government and Peace* (1993).

Introduction

by Dr. Harvey Sicherman

Situated as it is between Africa, Europe, and the Far East, the Middle East has played a unique role in world history. Often described as the birthplace of religions (notably Judaism, Christianity, and Islam) and the cradle of civilizations (Egypt, Mesopotamia, Persia), this region and its peoples have given humanity some of its most precious possessions. At the same time, the Middle East has had more than its share of conflicts. The area is strewn with the ruins of fortifications and the cemeteries of combatants, not to speak of modern arsenals for war.

Today, more than ever, Americans are aware that events in the Middle East can affect our security and prosperity. The United States has a considerable military, political, and economic presence throughout much of the region. Developments there regularly find their way onto the front pages of our newspapers and the screens of our television sets.

Still, it is fair to say that most Middle Eastern countries remain a mystery, their cultures and religions barely known, their peoples and politics confusing and strange. The purpose of this book series is to change that, to educate the reader in the basic facts about the 23 states and many peoples that make up the region. (For our purpose, the Middle East also includes the North African states linked by ethnicity, language, and religion to the Arabs, as well as Somalia and Mauritania, which are African but share the Muslim religion and are members of the Arab League.) A notable feature of the series is the integration of geography, demography, and history; economics and politics; culture and religion. The careful student will learn much that he or she needs to know about ever so important lands.

A few general observations are in order as an introduction to the subject matter.

The first has to do with history and politics. The modern Middle East is full of ancient sites and peoples who trace their lineage and literature to antiquity. Many commentators also attribute the Middle East's political conflicts to grievances and rivalries from the distant past. While history is often invoked, the truth is that the modern Middle East political system dates only from the 1920s and was largely created by the British and the French, the victors of World War I. Such states as Algeria, Iraq, Israel, Jordan, Kuwait, Saudi Arabia, Syria, Turkey, and the United Arab Emirates did not exist before 1914—they became independent between 1920 and 1971. Others, such as Egypt and Iran, were dominated by outside powers until well after World War II. Before 1914, most of the region's states were either controlled by the Turkish-run Ottoman Empire or owed allegiance to the Ottoman sultan. (The sultan was also the caliph or highest religious authority in Islam, in the line of the prophet Muhammad's successors, according to the beliefs of the majority of Muslims known as the Sunni.) It was this imperial Muslim system that was ended by the largely British military victory over the Ottomans in World War I. Few of the leaders who emerged in the wake of this event were happy with the territories they were assigned or the borders, which were often drawn by Europeans. Yet, the system has endured despite many efforts to change it.

The second observation has to do with economics, demography, and natural resources. The Middle Eastern peoples live in a region of often dramatic geographical contrasts: vast parched deserts and high mountains, some with year-round snow; stone-hard volcanic rifts and lush semi-tropical valleys; extremely dry and extremely wet conditions, sometimes separated by only a few miles; large permanent rivers and wadis, riverbeds dry as a bone until winter rains send torrents of flood from the mountains to the sea. In ancient times, a very skilled agriculture made the Middle East the breadbasket of the Roman Empire, and its trade carried luxury fabrics, foods, and spices both East and West.

Most recently, however, the Middle East has become more known for a single commodity—oil, which is unevenly distributed and largely concentrated in the Persian Gulf and Arabian Peninsula (although large pockets are also to be found in Algeria, Libya, and other sites). There are also new, potentially lucrative offshore gas fields in the Eastern Mediterranean.

This uneven distribution of wealth has been compounded by demographics. Birth rates are very high, but the countries with the most oil are often lightly populated. Over the last decade, Middle East populations under the age of 20 have grown enormously. How will these young people be educated? Where will they work? The failure of most governments in the region to give their people skills and jobs (with notable exceptions such as Israel) has also contributed to large out-migrations. Many have gone to Europe; many others work in other Middle Eastern countries, supporting their families from afar.

Another unsettling situation is the heavy pressure both people and industry have put on vital resources. Chronic water shortages plague the region. Air quality, public sanitation, and health services in the big cities are also seriously overburdened. There are solutions to these problems, but they require a cooperative approach that is sorely lacking.

A third important observation is the role of religion in the Middle East. Americans, who take separation of church and state for granted, should know that most countries in the region either proclaim their countries to be Muslim or allow a very large role for that religion in public life. Among those with predominantly Muslim populations, Turkey alone describes itself as secular and prohibits avowedly religious parties in the political system. Lebanon was a Christian-dominated state, and Israel continues to be a Jewish state. While both strongly emphasize secular politics, religion plays an enormous role in culture, daily life, and legislation. It is also important to recall that Islamic law (*Sharia*) permits people to prac-tice Judaism and Christianity in Muslim states but only as *Dhimmi*, protected but very second-class citizens.

Fourth, the American student of the modern Middle East will be impressed by the varieties of one-man, centralized rule, very unlike the workings of Western democracies. There are monarchies, some with traditional methods of consultation for tribal elders and even ordinary citizens, in Saudi Arabia and many Gulf States; kings with limited but still important parliaments (such as in Jordan and

Morocco); and military and civilian dictatorships, some (such as Syria) even operating on the hereditary principle (Hafez al Assad's son Bashar succeeded him). Turkey is a practicing democracy, although a special role is given to the military that limits what any government can do. Israel operates the freest democracy, albeit constricted by emergency regulations (such as military censorship) due to the Arab-Israeli conflict.

In conclusion, the MODERN MIDDLE EAST NATIONS series will engage imagination and interest simply because it covers an area of such great importance to the United States. Americans may be relative latecomers to the affairs of this region, but our involvement there will endure. We at the Foreign Policy Research Institute hope that these books will kindle a lifelong interest in the fascinating and significant Middle East.

The Pearl Monument (also known as the Gulf Cooperation Council Monument) symbolizes the importance pearl fishing once held in Bahrain. Today, there are many other things that make the tiny island country in the Arabian Gulf important, including its position as a strategic U.S. naval base.

Place in the World

The Kingdom of Bahrain consists of a group of 33 islands located on the western side of the Arabian Gulf between Saudi Arabia and the Qatar Peninsula. The largest of these islands is Bahrain, from which the country takes its name. Most of the country's population and infrastructure can be found on the island of Bahrain. In addition to Bahrain, four other islands are considered the kingdom's principal islands: Muharraq, Sitrah, Umm an-Nasan, and Nabi Salih. The remaining 27 islands are of lesser importance.

As a country made up of many small islands, it might seem that Bahrain would be a fragmented place with very little holding it together. Despite its small size (the country as a whole covers an area smaller than New York City) and its small population (at least 15 cities in the United States have populations greater than Bahrain's total), historically Bahrain has had an important influence on the Middle East.

Its position on trade routes has given the country a key role in international affairs. Bahrain is a place rich in culture. Its people are open and outgoing, and usually provide a warm welcome for foreigners.

ONE NATION, MANY RULERS

Bahrain has long been a place of economic and cultural importance in the Middle East. Its name means "two seas," which is appropriate given the fact that until relatively recently all trade to and from Bahrain was conducted via the sea.

The first inhabitants of the area now known as Bahrain were probably wanderers or exiles from an ancient Indus Valley civilization. In Bahrain these exiles established a civilization about 5,000 years ago. Their main city, Dilmun, thrived because of its advantageous position along the trade routes. Because of its location, however, Bahrain has been coveted by outside powers throughout history. At different times the powerful empires of the Sumerians, Babylonians, Persians, Greeks, Umayyads, Abbasids, Omanis, Portuguese, and Ottoman Turks have dominated the people of the islands.

In the 18th century, Great Britain entered into an arrangement with Bahrain similar to one the British had with other small kingdoms on the Arabian Peninsula known as the Trucial States (today, these make up the United Arab Emirates). Bahrain received British protection in exchange for allowing Britain to control the country's foreign policy. Britain also promised to protect local leaders from external and internal threats.

This relationship between Bahrain and Britain remained in place until 1971. However, Britain had never intended for these countries on the Arabian Gulf to be true colonial holdings. It had become involved in the region in order to protect the trade route to and from India, which had become an important British colony.

After India achieved independence from the British Empire in 1947, British leaders decided to extract themselves from a number of colonial situations, eventually withdrawing from all territories east of the Suez Canal.

Today, Bahrain is a **monarchy** ruled by King Hamad bin Isa bin Salman al-Khalifa. The Al Khalifa family first came to power in Bahrain in the 1780s, when they drove out the Persians with the help of Great Britain, and have ruled this nation ever since.

In the 1930s, Bahrain became the first Arab state in the Arabian Gulf region to develop an oil-based economy. While today Bahrain is not one of the largest producers of oil, in some ways this has worked to the country's advantage. Because Bahrain is unable to rely totally on its oil reserves to support its economy, it has expanded into other ventures, such as technology, textiles, and banking. Today, Bahrain is one of the largest banking centers in the Middle East.

A KEY U.S. ALLY

Bahrain has been an important strategic partner of the United States for more than 50 years. In 1949, when the country was still a British **protectorate**, the U.S. stationed a small group of ships in Bahrain. After 1971, when Bahrain became independent and the British withdrew their forces, the U.S. leased part of the former British naval station and expanded its presence in the region. Today, Bahrain is home to the U.S. Fifth Fleet, made up of some 25 warships and 15,000 sailors and marines.

The mission of the Fifth Fleet is to patrol the Arabian Gulf, Red Sea, Gulf of Oman, and Indian Ocean—an area of more than 7.5 million square miles that touches on such hot spots as Iran, Iraq, Pakistan, and Somalia. In the summer and fall of 1990 the Fifth Fleet carried out operations in support of United Nations sanctions against Iraq, which had invaded neighboring Kuwait in August.

U.S. Secretary of Defense Donald Rumsfeld meets with Bahrain's king, Hamad bin Isa al-Khalifa, at Sasfaria Palace. Bahrain is an important U.S. ally in the Gulf region and provides a base for the U.S. Fifth Fleet.

During the Gulf War, Bahrain served as the primary base for the naval forces of the 34-nation coalition that liberated Kuwait in the spring of 1991.

Today, the Fifth Fleet is based at Juffair, located five miles southeast of Manama, the capital and largest city of Bahrain. The U.S. Naval Support Activity (NSA) center occupies 79 acres of land in downtown Manama.

Since the September 11, 2001, terrorist attacks that destroyed the World Trade Center in New York City and damaged the Pentagon in Washington, D.C., Bahrain has cooperated with the United States in its war on terrorism. During Operation Enduring Freedom, carried out in late 2001 and 2002, Bahrain provided bases for U.S. aircraft bombing suspected terrorist camps in Afghanistan. When President George W. Bush announced a plan to freeze the financial assets of those suspected of terrorist activities, the Bahrain Monetary Agency took steps to prevent terrorists from transferring funds through the country's network of banks.

Bahrain has also cooperated with the U.S. in criminal investigations related to terrorist attacks. As a result, President Bush called Bahrain a major ally of the United States.

INTERNAL TENSION AND RELIGIOUS DIFFERENCES

Many Middle Eastern countries today are socially and politically unstable, and Bahrain is no different. One of the major divisions in the country is over religion. Although Islam is the state religion, and is practiced by about 85 percent of Bahrain's population, differences between two branches of the Muslim faith—Shiite and Sunni—have led to tension and violence.

The Sunni-Shiite split, a key event in the development of Islam, dates back to a few decades after the death of Muhammad, the prophet from Arabia who established the religion in the 7th century. After Muhammad's death in a.d. 632 his followers were divided over who would succeed him as the caliph, or leader, of the Muslims. Muhammad's only heir was his daughter, Fatimah, but according to Islamic law she was not eligible to succeed him because she was a woman. An assembly of Muhammad's advisors chose a man named Abu Bakr as the caliph. Although Abu Bakr was a close friend of Muhammad, as well as the father of Muhammad's second wife, he was not related to the prophet by blood. This indicated that the Islamic leader would be selected by the strength of his faith, not because he was related to Muhammad. Most Muslims agreed with this decision. Those who obeyed the caliphs are called Sunni Muslims.

A smaller group of Muslims disagreed. They felt that the caliph should be chosen from Muhammad's descendants, and believed Fatimah's husband Ali, who was also Muhammad's cousin, was the rightful caliph. They did not feel that Abu Bakr, or the two caliphs that followed him, were legitimate religious leaders. In 656 Ali was elected as the fourth caliph; however, he was murdered five years later. When Ali's son did not become caliph, Ali's followers, calling themselves Shiites, broke away from the rest of the faith.

The Shiite belief of *imamat* implies that after Muhammad, the only true leader of the Muslims is an imam. These are leaders descended from Muhammad through Ali, and thus believed to have been directly appointed by Allah. The Shiites recognized 12 imams, beginning with Ali and his sons Hassan and Hussein. The last of these imams, Muhammad al-Mahdi, is said to have ascended into heaven in 941; Shiites expect him to return as the Mahdi, or savior, at some time in the future.

Imams are considered *masoom* (meaning sinless and innocent) and therefore must be obeyed in all matters and under all circumstances. Thus *imams*, according to the beliefs of Shia Islam, are thus not just Muslim religious leaders, but political leaders as well.

Shiite Muslims mourn for Hussein, grandson of the Prophet Muhammad, during an annual three-day ceremony. Shiites are the majority in Bahrain, but the ruling Al Khalifa family follows Sunni Islam. This has caused tensions in the past and probably will continue to do so, as Bahrain moves toward democracy.

In recent years, the leadership qualities of the imam have been applied to the most learned men of the Shiite faith. This has enabled leaders like the Iranian cleric Ayatollah Ruholla Khomeini to seize power on both secular and religious grounds.

Today there are more than 1 billion Muslims worldwide. Of that number, Sunni Muslims make up more than 80 percent, while Shiites account for just about 15 percent. Bahrain is one of a few countries (Iran, Iraq, and Lebanon are the others) in which Shiites are the majority. In Bahrain it is estimated that 70 percent of the Muslim population follows Shia Islam. However, the ruling Al Khalifa family follows the Sunni branch of the faith. As long as the Al Khalifa family holds all of the power in Bahrain, and Shiites are denied an opportunity to participate in making laws and governing the country, tensions between the two groups will remain.

A MOVEMENT TOWARD DEMOCRACY

In recent years, Bahrain has moved toward democracy faster than any other Arab nation. In February 2002 the people of Bahrain approved a new constitution by an overwhelming margin. This established a National Assembly, which would be responsible for new legislation; the people of Bahrain—both men and women—can vote to determine half of the assembly's members, while the other half are appointed by the king, or emir. Although the Al Khalifa family remains in power, theoretically this assembly gives a measure of power to the people.

Elections to the National Assembly were held in the fall of 2002, and the assembly convened for the first time at the end of the year. Since then the eyes of the Arab world—and of the larger world as well—have been on Bahrain. Many people hope that if the small country's experiment with limited democracy is successful, other Middle Eastern countries will follow Bahrain's lead.

An aerial view of houses and shrublands on Bahrain Island. Bahrain had the reputation of being a lush land in the desert, and has remained more fertile than its neighbors on the Arabian Peninsula. However, the island's water supply is dwindling, which has forced the people of Bahrain to find creative ways to preserve this desert resource.

The Land

The Kingdom of Bahrain is an **archipelago** in the Arabian Gulf east of Saudi Arabia. Although the kingdom includes some 33 islands, most of the country's land area (approximately 90 percent) is found on Bahrain, the largest of the islands. The island of Bahrain is connected by **causeways** to Muharraq, the second largest island, and to Sitrah, which is primarily an industrial area. Other important islands are Nabi Salih, Jiddah (which houses the country's prison), and Umm an-Nasan (which houses a private **game preserve** and garden for the emir and his family).

The remaining islands of Bahrain are largely uninhabited, with the exception of the Hawar Islands off the coast of Qatar. These islands are best known for two reasons: the variety of migrating birds that pass through in spring and autumn, and the long-standing conflict between Bahrain and Qatar over which nation owns them. In March 2001, the International

Court of Justice in The Hague awarded possession of the islands to Bahrain.

The island of Bahrain is approximately 17 miles (27 kilometers) from the coast of Qatar and approximately 15 miles (24 km) from the coast of Saudi Arabia. Bahrain and Saudi Arabia are connected by the King Fahd Causeway, which was opened in 1986 and runs from Jasra, in northwest Bahrain, to al-Azizia, a suburb of Alkhobar in eastern Saudi Arabia. Customs and immigrations facilities are located on a man-made island in the center of the causeway.

Bahrain is a land that was once famous for its lush greenery—relatively speaking—in the middle of the Arab region's deserts. Natural springs once watered the island of Bahrain, irrigating the fertile northern and western areas. However, these springs have dried up, and increasing demands on the country's water supply are causing Bahrain to become less green. Today, water for drinking and irrigation is obtained from underground **aquifers**, or from **desalinization** plants in the kingdom.

The other islands that make up the Kingdom of Bahrain consist primarily of low, desert plains; there are no rivers, lakes, or other permanent bodies of water on these islands anymore.

The King Fahd Causeway, which links Bahrain to Saudi Arabia, was started in 1982 and completed in 1986. Construction of the four-lane highway cost $1.2 billion, and was financed by the Saudi government.

Geographically, all of Bahrain is low-lying desert land. The highest point in the entire country is just 400 feet (122 meters) above sea level.

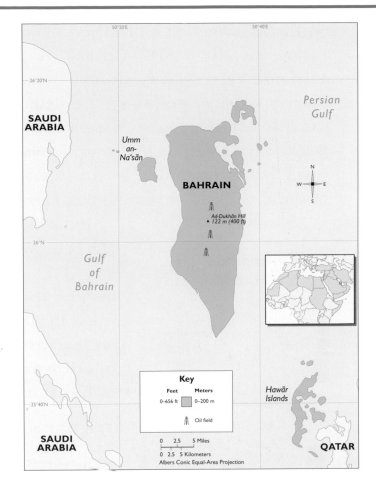

THE CLIMATE OF BAHRAIN

Bahrain's name is based on the Arabic phrase *thnain bahr*, meaning "two seas." This may refer to the phenomenon of sweet water springs under the ground that mingle with the salty water.

As one might expect of a desert nation, there is very little rainfall in Bahrain. The annual rainfall is less than four inches (10 centimeters), and this falls almost entirely during the winter months. At times, the annual rainfall has been known to fall all in one day and flood the streets, which are unprepared for this sudden volume of water. When the rain arrives, the desert comes alive with flowers and other vegetation.

Temperatures are coolest between December and March, when

northerly winds prevail. They often range from 50° to 68° Fahrenheit (10° to 20° Celsius). A prevailing wind, called the shammal, carries damp air over the archipelago of Bahrain from the southeast. Occasionally, the shammal brings a dust storm; it can also cause rough seas. A shammal can build up quickly and people often have very little warning or time to prepare. As a result, small fishing boats that go out to sea are usually equipped with powerful outboard motors so they can reach the shore in a hurry.

Humidity is high in July, August, and September, and temperatures average 96°F (36°C) during the summer months. Hot winds called *qaws* can cause the temperature to feel even hotter than usual, although a cooler wind, called *barra*, may at times relieve the high heat and humidity.

THE WATER PROBLEM

In the past the presence of ground water and natural springs have given Bahrain an advantage over its Arab neighbors on the desert mainland. The islands' supply of fresh water attracted trading ships to its harbors. Today, however, the supply of fresh water has been all but exhausted. Of the sweet water springs that once could be found throughout Bahrain, only the Adhari pool remains. Existing water wells are limited, and new **bore holes** can only be drilled after obtaining permission from the government. The Bahraini

Workers at a desalinization plant, where sea water is converted to drinking water.

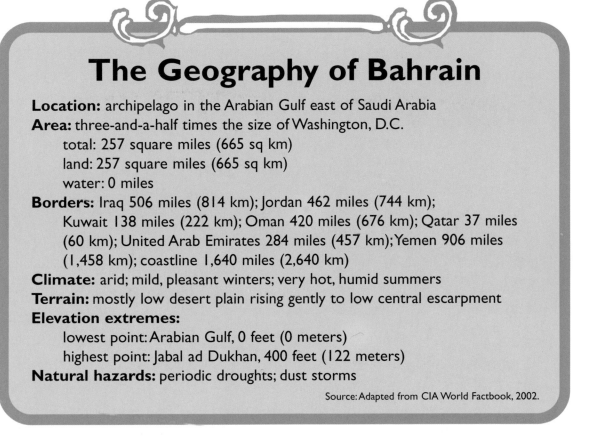

The Geography of Bahrain

Location: archipelago in the Arabian Gulf east of Saudi Arabia
Area: three-and-a-half times the size of Washington, D.C.
   total: 257 square miles (665 sq km)
   land: 257 square miles (665 sq km)
   water: 0 miles
Borders: Iraq 506 miles (814 km); Jordan 462 miles (744 km); Kuwait 138 miles (222 km); Oman 420 miles (676 km); Qatar 37 miles (60 km); United Arab Emirates 284 miles (457 km); Yemen 906 miles (1,458 km); coastline 1,640 miles (2,640 km)
Climate: arid; mild, pleasant winters; very hot, humid summers
Terrain: mostly low desert plain rising gently to low central escarpment
Elevation extremes:
   lowest point: Arabian Gulf, 0 feet (0 meters)
   highest point: Jabal ad Dukhan, 400 feet (122 meters)
Natural hazards: periodic droughts; dust storms

Source: Adapted from CIA World Factbook, 2002.

government is careful to ensure that the establishment of a new well will not take water away from an existing one, and is therefore reluctant to grant permission for any new wells.

Freshwater can be taken from underground aquifers, but this is a non-renewable resource because of the lack of rain in the region. As more and more freshwater is withdrawn from the underground aquifers, salt water from the Arabian Gulf seeps into the aquifers, making the groundwater brackish.

Every person in Bahrain uses dozens of gallons of water each day for drinking, bathing, washing clothes and dishes, and watering gardens and yards. To provide enough water for everyday use, the government has invested in desalinization plants. Desalinization is the process of removing the salt from seawater so

Bahrainis have always regarded water as a gift from the gods, and there is an ancient legend explaining how this desert nation came to have an abundance of such a precious commodity. Falling stars must have knocked holes in the ground, it is said, and Allah filled them with water for the use of his faithful followers.

that it can be used for human and animal consumption. However, desalinization is very expensive.

There are environmental problems that affect the quality of Bahrain's water as well. Oil spills and other discharges from large tankers, oil refineries, and distribution stations have damaged coastlines, coral reefs, and sea vegetation along Bahrain and the Arabian Gulf coast. Furthermore, in some areas industrial pollutants have contaminated water sources with heavy metals. All this has caused agricultural development to be neglected, and the limited amount of arable land in Bahrain has been degraded. In addition, erosion of farmland has brought further desertification.

There are acres of land that could be converted to fertile farmland, if there was access to water. However, successful agriculture requires such a large amount of fresh water that the cost of desalinizing and transporting the water to the areas where it is needed would be prohibitive. The government does not want to pay these extra costs. Instead, it has searched for other solutions.

One program that seems to have worked is in the city of Tubli, where **sewerage** was constructed as part of an environmental improvement program. The system was inspected to see if the **effluent** could be processed to remove harmful waste and then used to irrigate farmland. This would solve two problems at once: farms could get the water they so desperately needed, and the processing would help clean up the environment, particularly the coastal waters around Bahrain. It also would be less costly than shipping water to the city for farming.

The project has been a success. Tests show that the water not only falls within the recommended limits for irrigation water, it is actually safe enough to be used as drinking water. This and other creative programs to conserve water have enabled agriculture to succeed in Bahrain; today, the country produces more than 75 percent of the fruits and vegetables its population consumes.

In the meantime, the government has continued to invest in other water projects. A $360 million expansion of the al-Hidd power and desalinization facility, located on Muharraq Island, is currently underway; when it is finished in 2005 the facility should be able to increase production of fresh water by 30 percent. At the same time, farmers in Bahrain began using a product that could be added to sandy soil to help it retain moisture. This soil enhancer, Fytofoam, was tested in 2001 by Bahrain's Works and Agriculture Ministry, which found that when used properly the product could reduce the amount of water needed for farming by 70 percent.

Despite these efforts, water remains a critical issue in Bahrain.

WELL-SUITED PLANTS AND ANIMALS

In spite of the fact that Bahrain has a desert environment, the islands are home to a variety of plant and animal life. Many plants are halophytes (plants that are salt-tolerant) and xerophytes (plants that are drought-resistant), which enable them to survive in a land where there is little fresh water.

There are many date palm trees, although increased groundwater salinity has reduced their numbers. In older written records, Bahrain was referred to as the "land of a million palms." Bahrainis consider the date palm tree to have been blessed by God with qualities not found in other trees. This is because of the tree's amazing versatility. Every part of it can be used for something: the dates provide food for people and animals; the trunk and branch-es can be used to build anything from houses to boats to fish traps; the leaves are used to make mats, fans, and baskets; the fibers are used to make ropes; and the wood is used for fuel.

Aside from donkeys and camels (which are actually **imported** into the region and are not native to the desert island), the land animals in Bahrain include desert rats, gazelles, mongooses, lizards, snakes, and rabbits. Bird life includes larks, swallows, bulbuls (a type of songbird related to the nightingale), parakeets, and thrushes.

The government funds a conservation program to breed the endangered white (or Arabian) oryx, a type of antelope, at

A Bahraini man uses a net to collect fish caught in a trap at low tide, near Manama. The waters of the Gulf around Bahrain are rich in marine life.

al-Areen Wildlife Park, near al-Markh. Zebras have recently been introduced to the park and have been thriving alongside the Arabian oryx. Other goals of the park include planting trees and vegetation to positively affect the environment, encouraging the successful breeding of rare animal species, and providing a recreational and educational facility for visitors.

The marine life in the Arabian Gulf around Bahrain is more varied than the life on land. Grouper, mackerel, shrimp, pearl oysters, and dugongs (sea cows) all live in Bahrain's coastal waters.

In the southern part of Bahrain Island, in a largely deserted dry patch of ground, there stands a single tree. No one is certain how this tree has managed to live without water in the desert; it may be watered by an underground spring. It is called the Tree of Life, and some people believe it is an indication that the biblical Garden of Eden was once located in Bahrain.

القرآن ثم أربعاً بعد أساطيرها وخارف جلّاها وقال اركبوا فيها بسم الله مجراها
ومرساها ثمّ نفّس نفس المغرمين أو عباد الله المكرمين وقال له أما انا

This page from a 13th-century Arabic manuscript shows a dhow, a vessel commonly used by Arab sailors in the Indian Ocean. Because of its strategic location in the Arabian Gulf, Bahrain was an ancient trading center.

History

For much of its history, Bahrain has been at the center of either trade or conflict. Other nations or empires have sought to control Bahrain because of its strategic position and its resources.

It is thought that the area now known as Bahrain was first inhabited more than 5,200 years ago. Sometime after 3000 B.C. a great Bronze Age trading empire was established on the island, the Dilmun civilization. Dilmun played a key role in ancient trade because of its strategic location between Mesopotamia (in present-day southern Iraq) and the civilizations of the Indus Valley (present-day India and Pakistan). Clay tablets with **cuneiform** writing indicate that Dilmun was about two days sailing distance from Mesopotamia, and sailors stopped regularly to load fresh food and water onto their ships.

From 2100 to 1700 b.c., Dilmun was a major city, prob-

These ancient ruins date back to the Dilmun civilization, a trading empire that flourished on Bahrain more than 3,500 years ago.

ably containing a population of between 2,000 to 4,000 people. Adventurers from Dilmun sailed their ships, called dhows, through the waters of the Arabian Gulf, the Red Sea, and the Indian Ocean. Not everyone made a living from trade, however. There were many farmers on Bahrain. In the relatively shallow coastal waters, pearlers would dive as deep as 75 feet (23 meters) to gather the rare gems. The island had a shipbuilding industry, and there was also a profitable industry in the collection of aromatic gum from the frankincense and myrrh bushes. These were used in religious ceremonies, funeral rites, and for medicinal purposes.

In addition to being a prosperous trading center, Dilmun was also considered a sacred place. In what is now the northwest corner of Bahrain are the remains of five temple complexes. One ancient manuscript says that the island was a place where the people did not grow old, and where there was no fighting.

Interestingly, more than 170,000 burial mounds can be found dotting the desert landscape, making Bahrain the location of one of the largest prehistoric graveyards in the world. Some of the mounds are just bumps on the ground, but others are as high as 40 feet. If these burial mounds had been preserved intact, they would have provided a wealth of evidence about the lives and civilization of the ancient Dilmun people. Unfortunately, over the past 3,000 years grave robbers have pillaged the mounds, stealing or destroying many clues to the past that the burial sites might have provided. However, modern-day ***archaeologists*** have found weapons, objects made of copper and bronze, jewelry, and vases from Egypt, Mesopotamia, Oman, and the Indus Valley.

A PERIOD OF FOREIGN RULE

From about 1700 B.C. to 700 A.D., a number of foreign powers exerted control over Bahrain. In each case, as the conquering civilization arrived Bahrain suffered economically at first, but eventually regained its place as a key center of trade.

Around 1700 B.C., the Assyrians asserted control over the Gulf region. This powerful empire had risen from northern Mesopotamia, and eventually controlled a huge area stretching from the Mediterranean Sea to the Caspian Sea and from the Red Sea to the Arabian Gulf. At its height, the Assyrian Empire was larger than any ancient empire that preceded it. Many records detail the accomplishments of Assyrian rulers, but little is known about the everyday life of ordinary people.

As the Assyrian Empire declined, a new power rose in Mesopotamia. The Babylonians eventually conquered the Assyrians, and absorbed Bahrain around 600 B.C. They remained in control of the region until the Persians, from present-day Iran, conquered Babylon in the sixth century B.C. and made Bahrain a part of the powerful Persian empire.

Around 325 B.C., the Macedonian conqueror Alexander the Great sent a Greek fleet into the Arabian Gulf. Nearchus, an admiral in Alexander's navy, established a small colony on one of the Gulf islands (now part of Kuwait). Under the Greeks, Bahrain became known as Tylos. After Alexander's death, the empire was divided among four of his generals; a general named Seleucus took control of the region that includes Bahrain. During the rule of Seleucus and his descendants (known as the Seleucids), Bahrain, Syria, Mesopotamia, and Persia enjoyed a measure of prosperity. However, by 250 B.C. the Parthians, another powerful empire from Persia, had forced the Greeks from the Gulf region.

In the third century A.D., Persian control of the Gulf region reached its highest point under the rule of the Sassanids, a Persian *dynasty*. The Sassanids ruled the area for about four centuries.

During this time, several religions were introduced to Bahrain. Judaism had been permitted by the Sassanids, and Jews traveled to Bahrain from the Arabian Desert and from Mesopotamia. Christianity arrived in the region as early as the first century A.D., and its practice had become more widespread by the start of the fifth century. However, the dominant religion of the region was Zoroastrianism (today called Parsee). This Persian religion was founded around 1000 B.C. by a man named Zoroaster (sometimes spelled Zarathustra). The religion's core belief is that the universe is involved in a struggle between the forces of good (Ormuzd) and evil (Ahriman). Ultimately, Ormuzd will prevail, in part with the help of man, whom he created to strengthen his forces. Zoroaster established three commandments—good thoughts, good words, good deeds.

In the early seventh century, the Byzantine Empire drove the Sassanids from their eastern Arabian outposts. The Byzantines

Foreign dignitaries bring tribute, in the form of gifts, to Persian ruler Darius I, in a relief dating from the Achaemenid period (553–330 B.C.). Through most of Bahrain's history, the islands of modern-day Bahrain were under Persian control; even today, the culture of Persia (today called Iran) has a great influence on the people of Bahrain.

were the eastern half of the Roman Empire, which had split in 395 A.D. Though the western part of the empire fell in the fifth century, the Byzantines remained powerful. This Christian empire was based in the city of Constantinople in modern-day Turkey. However, Byzantine control of the Gulf region would not last long, as a galvanizing new religion, Islam, was rising in the east.

NEW RELIGION, NEW RULERS

By 650, the entire Arabian Peninsula had come under the rule of the followers of the Prophet Muhammad, founder of Islam. Muhammad had been born around the year 570 A.D., and was a

The prophet Muhammad ascends to heaven on a human-faced steed in this 16th-century illustration attributed to a Persian artist. Muhammad's revelations from Allah became the basis of a new religion, Islam, which swept across the Arabian Peninsula in the 7th century.

prosperous trader in the city of Mecca, in modern-day Saudi Arabia. Like many people who lived in the desert at this time, Muhammad was **polytheistic**, meaning he believed in a number of gods. When he was about 40 years old, Muhammad received a visit from an angel, who explained that there was only one God, Allah, and told the trader to spread this message to the world.

Muhammad began preaching this belief, and soon attracted a group of followers. However, the authorities in Mecca did not like what he had to say, and in 622 Muhammad was forced to leave the city. However, his beliefs continued to draw disciples. In 629 he returned to Mecca with an army and forced the city to surrender; after this most of the people of Mecca accepted Muhammad's beliefs. By the time of Muhammad's death in 632, there were thousands of followers of the new religion, which became known as Islam.

The Muslims, or followers of Islam, were not afraid to use force to spread their beliefs. By 650 A.D., the new religion had spread throughout the Arabian Peninsula, and by the end of the century Muslim Arabs had taken control of the Middle East and North Africa from the Byzantine Empire. During the next seven centuries, Bahrain was under the control of two powerful Islamic dynasties— the Umayyad, which lasted from 661 to around 750, and the Abbasid, which held power from 750 to 1258.

The Islamic faith was not united during this time; the split between the Sunni and Shiite Muslims occurred in 661, and fighting between the two groups continued until Ali's son Hussein, considered by Shiites the third imam, was killed at the battle of Karbala in 680 by the forces of Yazin, a Sunni caliph of the Umayyad dynasty. After this Sunnis held most of the power, while the Shiites were forced into a minority role.

The Umayyad caliphs ruled first from Damascus (in present-day Syria) and later from Baghdad (in Iraq). After the rise of the

Abbasids, the center of power in the Islamic world shifted to Iran. During the rule of these powerful dynasties, therefore, Bahrain and other lands in the Arabian Gulf region were near the center of the Islamic world. As a result, the people of Bahrain prospered. Merchants and sailors from Bahrain and other Gulf States such as Oman continued to ply the Indian Ocean, with some sailing thousands of miles to the eastern coast of China. Arab traders were instrumental in spreading Islam to India, Malaysia, Indonesia, and along the east coast of Africa.

During the rule of the Abbasid dynasty, a small group of Muslims living on Bahrain gained a lot of power in the region for a short time. In the ninth century, a group of Shiites broke away from other Shiites over a dispute about the rightful succession of the imamate. The sixth Shiite imam, Jafar al-Sadiq, had appointed his eldest son, Ismail, to follow him as imam; however, when Ismail died before his father, Jafar al-Sadiq named his second son, Musa, as imam. Most Shiites accepted this decision when Jafar al-Sadiq died in 765, but some felt that succession of the imamate should go through Ismail's family. They separated from the Shiite community and became known as Ismailis.

The Ismailis established a tradition of sending missionaries to explain their faith and to create Ismaili communities. One of these missionaries was Hamdan Qarmat, who sent a group to establish an Ismaili community on Bahrain around 877. The Ismailis of Bahrain, who became known as the Qarmatians, were soon among the strongest tribes in the region, and remained so for most of the tenth century. In 930 they sacked Mecca and Medina. Other Ismaili groups controlled the coast of Oman, raided Syria and Iraq, exacted tribute from their neighbors, and sent missionaries throughout the Muslim world. Ismaili power in the Bahrain area was broken by the might of the Persians by 988. However, other Ismailis eventually created the Fatamid dynasty, which ruled in

Egypt and North Africa between the 10th and 12th centuries.

After the collapse of the Abbasid dynasty in the mid-13th century, Bahrain entered a long, turbulent period, during which it often found itself in the middle of affairs between its more powerful neighbors. Soon new powers would begin to involve themselves in the Gulf region.

THE ARRIVAL OF THE EUROPEANS

While the Arab civilization of Bahrain was flourishing under the rule of the Umayyads and Abbasids, many changes were occurring thousands of miles away in Europe. Although these events did not directly affect the people of the islands around Bahrain, they would ultimately lead to the arrival of Europeans in the Gulf region in the 16th century. The effect of European involvement in the region can be felt today.

After the fall of the Roman Empire in 476, Europe had fallen into the Dark Ages. During this time many aspects of civilization were destroyed or forgotten. The great works of Greek and Roman scholars were lost. Few people could read or write; most scratched out a meager living on small farms. It was a difficult, dangerous time to be alive.

At the same time, in the Middle East the Arabic civilization was flourishing. Arabic scholars preserved the writings of the ancient Greeks and Romans, and contributed to human knowledge of mathematics, science, astronomy, and other areas of learning. Arabs from North Africa even spread their civilization into Europe, invading the Iberian Peninsula in the eighth century and conquering much of modern-day Spain and Portugal.

The differences between Muslim Arabs and European Christians eventually led to a series of religious wars. These wars, known as the Crusades, were fought to recapture Jerusalem, and other sites in the Middle East considered holy to Christians, from

Muslim control. The first Crusade was launched in 1095, and the fighting continued until the last Crusaders were killed or forced to leave the Holy Land in 1291.

At the same time, Christians on the Iberian Peninsula fought to rid their country of the Moors, the Arab invaders from North Africa. These efforts were gradually successful. By 1065, a Christian ruler known as Ferdinand the Great had forced the Moors from the northwestern Iberian Peninsula and reorganized the territories into the kingdom of Portugal. Others followed Ferdinand's lead and battled the Muslims. The *Reconquista* was completed in 1492, when troops sent by King Ferdinand of Aragon and Queen Isabella of Castile forced the Muslims from their last stronghold on the peninsula, the city of Grenada. (Aragon and Castille had been united after the 1469 marriage of Ferdinand and Isabella; ultimately the kingdom of León also joined the union to create the modern-day state of Spain.)

Christians had been fighting Muslims for hundreds of years. Yet the accomplishments of the Arab civilization—introduced to Europeans during the Crusades and the period of Moorish occupation of the Iberian Peninsula—had helped to pull Europe out of the Dark Ages. Ancient books were rediscovered in Arabic libraries in such Spanish centers of learning as Andalusia and Córdoba. In addition, items from the Middle East and Far East regions, such as fine silk cloth, beautiful jewelry and precious stones, and rare spices like pepper, cinnamon, and nutmeg, became highly valued in Europe. Merchants like the 13th-century traveler Marco Polo established trade routes to China along which these valuables could be brought to European markets.

However, by the 15th century a new power had risen in the east—the Ottoman Turks. The Turks made it dangerous for caravans to travel the Silk Road, the land route linking Europe to India and China. The only source for spices and other goods from the

East was Arab traders who brought the goods across the Mediterranean to Italian cities like Venice and Genoa. Those who wanted to eliminate these middlemen and trade directly with the East had to find another way.

In 1420 a prince of Portugal who has become known as Henry the Navigator began sending expeditions south along the coast of Africa. His ultimate goal was to find a sea route around the continent, by which Portuguese ships could reach Asia. At the time, of course, geographic knowledge was limited and no one knew whether such a route existed. Henry died long before his dream was fulfilled, but others continued his work. In 1497–98, a Portuguese captain named Vasco da Gama led an expedition that rounded the southern tip of Africa and headed north. With the help of Arab sailors from East Africa, Gama was able to cross the Indian Ocean and reach Calicut, where he established a trade agreement with the ruler before returning home in 1499.

The Portuguese had their trade route; next, they had to defend their ships from attacks by Arab merchants, who did not want the Portuguese cutting them out of the lucrative spice trade with Europe. Portugal sent armed warships and soldiers; by 1511 the Portuguese had captured numerous cities from the Arabs and controlled the Indian Ocean.

The Portuguese ultimately widened their sphere of influence into the Arabian Gulf region. They captured coastal cities in Oman and Persia, and forced local rulers to pay tribute to Portugal. In 1521, the Portuguese occupied Bahrain. The main Portuguese fleet was stationed near the Strait of Hormuz, in present-day Oman. While in the region, the Portuguese built Arad Fort on Muharraq Island, in order to control local and foreign opposition to their rule.

Though Persia had been the major presence in the region before the arrival of the Portuguese, during the 16th century the country was weakened by Portugal's presence in the Gulf, as well as by attacks in the west by the Ottoman Turks. In 1588 a new ruler, Shah Abbas I, came to power in Persia determined to change this. He negotiated peace agreements with the Ottomans, then decided to seek help to resist Portugal. Abbas invited the British and Dutch into the region; he offered them half the revenue from Persian ports if they would force out the Portuguese. Both countries agreed. The British would ultimately have the greater influence in the Gulf region, as the Dutch concentrated on taking over Portuguese colonies in the Indian Ocean. In 1622 a combined British-Persian force drove the Portuguese out of Arad Fort and their other strongholds on the Strait of Hormuz, ending Portugal's control over Bahrain.

Portuguese ships attack an Arab dhow during the early 16th century. When the Portuguese arrived in the Arabian Gulf region, their ships were armed with cannons. This gave them a great advantage over the Arab sailors. The dhows did not have cannons; instead, the Arabs fought by ramming enemy ships and boarding them with soldiers to overwhelm the crews. By 1521 the Portuguese controlled much of the coastal areas around the Arabian Gulf and Indian Ocean, including Bahrain.

The remains of a Portuguese fort in Bahrain, near Manama. Two earlier forts have been discovered nearby, one dating back to the time of the Seleucids and the other built in the sixth century. The Portuguese ruled Bahrain until they were pushed out by the Persians and the British in the early 17th century.

To a degree, the British remained involved in the Gulf region. However, for most of the next 160 years Bahrain was dominated by Persia. This domination was usually exercised through Arab **vassals**.

In 1718, the armies of the **sultan** of Oman seized Bahrain from the Persians; they held it until 1737, when Persia recaptured it. Over the next five decades, several sheikhs fought for control of the islands. In 1783, the Al Khalifa family took control, establishing a ruling dynasty that remains in power today.

DEVELOPMENT OF THE KINGDOM

The Al Khalifa family had arrived in Bahrain during the mid-18th century. They were members of a tribe of **nomadic** desert-dwellers called the Bani Utub, who had moved from central Arabia to Kuwait. There, the Al Khalifas had helped another Bani Utub family, the al Sabah, establish a settlement near present-day Kuwait City. After leaving Kuwait, the Al Khalifas had settled on the northwestern coast of Qatar, but in the early 1780s, under the leadership of Sheikh Ahmed bin Muhammad al-Khalifa (also known as Ahmed al-Fatih, the conqueror), they drove the Persians out of Bahrain and occupied the principal islands.

Turkish forces attack Constantinople, 1453. The fall of the city marked the end of the Byzantine Empire and the rise of a new power, the Ottoman Turks. However, although the Ottoman Empire claimed to rule the entire Arabian Peninsula and Persia, it never established control over Bahrain. The islands, along with the Trucial States along the coast and parts of central Arabia, were the only areas of the Middle East not to fall under Turkish control during the more than 500 years of Ottoman rule. Instead, Great Britain was the major imperial influence on Bahrain during most of the 17th to the 20th centuries.

Bahrain remained near the center of pressure from powerful outside forces. By the late 18th century the Ottoman Empire was attempting to exert influence over the region from Iraq. Persia also remained a force to be reckoned with in the Gulf. On the Strait of Hormuz, the al-bu-Said family had wrested control of Oman from the Persians and were attempting to expand their influence in the region. And Great Britain was becoming more involved in Arab affairs to protect its interests in the area—the British had made India part of their empire during the mid-18th century. The British not only wanted to protect its ships along the trade routes, they also wanted to limit the influence of rival powers, such as the Ottoman Turks and the French, in the Arabian Gulf.

In 1794, Ahmed al-Fatih died and his son Salman took control of Bahrain. However, his rule was interrupted when Oman invaded the islands. Help from Great Britain enabled Salman and his brother Abdulla to regain control of Bahrain. In return, they signed a trade treaty with the British East India Company. After Salman died in 1821, Abdulla signed another treaty with the British in which he agreed not to allow pirates to operate from the islands. In return, Great Britain helped the Al Khalifa family to strengthen their control over the land.

After Sheikh Abdulla died in 1842, power passed to Salman's son Muhammad, who ruled until 1867. While he was in power, he signed the "Treaty of Perpetual Peace and Friendship" with the British.

After Muhammad's death, his brother Ali became the sheikh, but a struggle for power ensued. Rival factions sought control of the country, Ali was assassinated, and the son of former Sheikh Abdulla took control. In late 1869, however, the British stepped in and placed Ali's 21-year-old son, Isa, on the throne, exiling his rivals.

The rule of Sheikh Isa bin Ali al-Khalifa from 1869 to 1932 marked the beginning of a stable period in Bahrain's history. The sheikh introduced new administrative and legal institutions and laid the foundations of Bahrain's modern system of education. During his reign, Bahrain's first bank and post office were opened and a telegraph station was installed, linking Bahrain to the rest of the world. And in the last years of his reign a substance was discovered that would ensure Bahrain's importance in the world for years to come—oil. Oil revenues would eventually enable Bahrain to establish itself as a modern nation. Some of the money would be used to build schools, hospitals, and government buildings; the sheikhs also constructed power plants, strung telephone lines, and provided other services to the people throughout the islands.

During the rule of Isa bin Ali, Great Britain signed an agreement with the Ottoman Empire in 1913, in which the

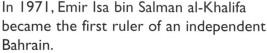

In 1971, Emir Isa bin Salman al-Khalifa became the first ruler of an independent Bahrain.

Ottomans recognized the independence of Bahrain. However, the country would remain firmly under the control of the British for the next six decades.

BAHRAIN GAINS INDEPENDENCE

Bahrain remained a protectorate of Great Britain until 1968, when Britain announced that it was withdrawing its presence from the region, a process that would be complete in 1971. This announcement came as quite a shock to the rulers of the small Arab nations of the Gulf region, including Bahrain. They liked the protection their arrangement with the British provided, and were sorry to see things change. Although Britain had a strong influence in Bahrain's government and policies—at least as the country related to the rest of the world—internal, day-to-day government affairs were left largely to local leaders. It was an arrangement that suited both countries equally well.

Once the British established their timetable for departing, the Arab states in the region began to discuss their future. Bahrain considered a proposal to form a federation with Qatar and the seven Trucial States (now known as the United Arab Emirates, or UAE). When the other nations refused to agree to Bahrain's demand that it receive greater representation on the council that would govern this federation, Bahrain declared its independence alone on August 14, 1971, under the rule of an emir, or king, Isa bin Salman al-Khalifa. Qatar followed suit on September 3, 1971. Six of the Trucial States formed the United Arab Emirates and declared independence on December 2, 1971; a seventh state joined the federation the next year.

Economically, Bahrain fared well because of its oil revenues. These increased dramatically in 1973–74 when the worldwide price of oil rose sharply because of an embargo by the Arab members of the Organization of Petroleum Exporting Countries (OPEC). The

OPEC embargo, a response to Western support of Israel during the 1973 Yom Kippur War with Egypt and Syria, raised the price of a barrel of crude oil from $3 to $12. Bahrain used the resulting increase in oil revenues to begin development projects throughout the country.

THE FIRST CONSTITUTION

On December 16, 1971, Bahrain formally became independent of Great Britain. That day, Emir Isa bin Salman al-Khalifa announced that Bahrain would adopt a constitution. This, he hoped, would solidify Bahraini society and encourage a greater level of participation in the political affairs of the islands.

The emir decided to establish a national constitutional assembly consisting of both appointed and elected members. In theory, this would represent all aspects of society. In June 1972, the emir issued a decree for the election of 22 Bahrainis to the assembly, which would also include 20 members who were either appointed by the emir or were members of his Council of Ministers. The assembly would be charged with creating and **ratifying** a new constitution. The election was held in December 1972—the first democratic election in the country's history, although only native-born male citizens over the age of 20 were allowed to vote.

Among Bahrain's citizens, opinions on the idea of a constitution were divided. Some supported the idea, while others felt it was merely a means of legitimizing the existing political system, in which the ruler merely consulted with the people before making decisions. Bahraini women organized demonstrations in the streets to protest their exclusion from the electoral process.

After meeting for most of 1973, the constitutional assembly produced a document with 108 articles. Although the constitution ensured that a member of the Al Khalifa family would remain the country's ruler, among its provisions was the establishment of a

National Assembly. This assembly would consist of 30 members elected to four-year terms as well as the members of the Council of Ministers, who were appointed by the emir to run various departments of government. The assembly would not have the power to create laws, but it could become involved in debates over the laws and policies created by the Council of Ministers. This was a small step toward representative democracy, but a step nonetheless. However, the assembly would serve at the discretion of the emir, who had the power to dissolve it at any time.

Elections for this assembly were held in December 1973; again, only male citizens were allowed to vote. Political parties were outlawed, so technically all of the elected members of the assembly were independents. However, some of the 30 elected members soon gravitated into voting blocs. One eight-member coalition, known as the People's Bloc, advocated traditional labor demands—the right to establish unions, greater participation in economic policymaking, and higher wages. These representatives also wanted the government to repeal the 1965 Law of Public Security. This was a series of decrees that gave the emir dictatorial power to protect the country from foreign enemies or domestic unrest. His broad powers essentially meant that anyone could be arrested and held without trial on suspicion of crimes against the state.

A second group of six Shiite representatives formed the Religious Bloc. They supported the labor reforms advocated by the People's Bloc, but wanted these measures to be tied to the implementation of strict regulations, based in Islamic law, on various aspects of Bahraini life, such as restrictions on the sale of alcoholic beverages and interaction between men and women in public places.

The other 16 elected members of the assembly shifted their positions from issue to issue, often trying to facilitate compromises between the two voting blocs and the Council of Ministers.

The people of Bahrain were very interested in the assembly, and its debates on national government, laws, and policy. Even though the assembly had little power, the emir and his ministers felt the public debates were undermining their government. In June 1975, Bahrain's prime minister announced that the Council of Ministers would resign from the National Assembly. Two months later, the emir formally dissolved the National Assembly and reinstated the cabinet, giving it "full legislative powers." Although the constitution had required new elections within two months if the emir dissolved the assembly, they were never held. Bahrain's experiment with democracy had ended.

UNREST IN THE REGION

After dissolving the assembly, Bahrain's government had to deal with internal unrest, particularly among the country's Shiite population. Although Shiites make up a majority of the population, in general they were poorer than Sunni citizens of Bahrain. In addition, because the ruling family and members of the Cabinet of Ministers followed the Sunni branch of the faith, Shiites felt discriminated against by the government.

Events outside of Bahrain during the late 1970s contributed to instability within the country, and in the Gulf region as a whole. Most notable was the 1979 revolution in Iran led by the Ayatollah Ruholla Khomeini, which established a fundamentalist government that was based on a strict interpretation of Islamic law and controlled by Shiite religious leaders.

Khomeini had been denouncing the Iranian government of Shah Mohammad Reza Pahlevi since the 1950s, when the shah had asked the United States for help during a revolt by Iranian Shiites seeking democratic reform. In 1964 Khomeini was exiled to Turkey. He was later allowed to move to the Shiite holy city of An Najaf, Iraq, where he continued preaching against the Shah's rule. During his exile Khomeini also started a movement to establish a fundamentalist Islamic state in Iran. As a *Time* magazine profile by Milton Viorst explains:

> In An Najaf, Khomeini also shaped a revolutionary doctrine. Shi'ism, historically, demanded of the state only that it keep itself open to clerical guidance. Though relations between clergy and state were often tense, they were rarely belligerent. Khomeini, condemning the Shah's servility to America and his secularism, deviated from accepted tenets to attack the regime's legitimacy, calling for a clerical state, which had no Islamic precedent.

In January 1978, a pro-Khomeini demonstration took place in Qom, a city in central Iran considered sacred by Shiites. When Iranian police intervened, the demonstration turned into a riot. About 70 people were killed before the violence ended. From exile, Khomeini called on Shiites to hold memorial services on the 40th day after their deaths. These memorials, which followed Islamic custom, were held across the nation. Unrest at a service in Tabríz, Iran, led to new riots and more fatalities. This led to a cycle of nationwide mourning services every 40 days, several of which turned violent and led to more deaths.

Tensions between the people and the government grew even higher after the shah imposed martial law on Tehran and 11 other cities in July 1978. In

The Iranian Shiite leader Ayatollah Ruholla Khomeini opposed the government of the shah, accusing it of being corrupt and subordinate to Western influences.

protest, workers left their jobs. Within two months, this general strike had paralyzed Iran's economy.

By the fall of 1978, a unified revolutionary movement had evolved. From Iraq, Khomeini continued to preach against what he saw as the corruption and injustices of the shah's regime. After the shah persuaded Iraq to expel Khomeini from the country, the Shiite leader found asylum in Paris, France. This turned out to be a good move for Khomeini, as he could now spread the message to his followers with the help of the international media. By November, it was clear that the Iranian government could not

During 1978, protests and mourning services led to violent clashes with the Shah's police. These eventually led to the overthrow of the shah and institution of a theocratic government headed by Khomeini. Unrest in Iran concerned the leaders of Iran's Arab neighbors—particularly the rulers of Bahrain because of the island's majority Shiite population.

endure. The shah left the country in January 1979, traveling to the United States for medical treatment. He would never return to Iran. By the end of February Khomeini had returned in triumph and the shah's government was overthrown. On April 1, Iranians voted to establish a **theocratic** government headed by Khomeini.

Iran's Islamic revolution increased tensions between Sunnis and Shiites in Bahrain. Shiites in Bahrain sympathized with and supported their fellow believers in Iran. Iran's aggressive stance toward the nations of the West contributed to the division between the governments of Bahrain and Iran. Khomeini called the United States "the Great Satan," and in November 1979 Iranians stormed the U.S. Embassy in Tehran, capturing more than 50 Americans and holding them hostage for over a year.

In 1981 and 1985, the Bahraini authorities foiled Shiite plots—allegedly supported by the Iranian government—to overthrow the Al Khalifa government. Iran denied official involvement in the plots. However, even if Iran was not directly involved, at the very least Khomeini had inspired the attempts at revolution with his constant exhortations to Shiites to spread the Islamic revolution throughout the Gulf region.

Iran, with its population of more than 60 million and its arsenal of weapons, would be a formidable enemy, and the small Arab states of the Gulf region felt vulnerable. To protect themselves, Bahrain, Kuwait, Oman, Qatar, Saudi Arabia, and the states of the UAE formed the Gulf Cooperation Council (GCC) in May 1981. This was an agreement for mutual defense of the region, but also provided for the countries to work together economically.

The Gulf region would remain unstable throughout the 1980s. A war between Iran and Iraq began in September 1980, and continued until 1988. Although Bahrain and the other Gulf states tried to remain neutral, when military aircraft attacked oil tankers belonging to Kuwait and Saudi Arabia in the Arabian Gulf in 1986, they

Emir Hamad bin Isa al-Khalifa holds up a copy of Bahrain's national charter in February 2002. The new document established the kingdom as a constitutional monarchy and provided for the election of a national assembly.

threw their support behind Iraq, which is also an Arab country. Iran then began a secret campaign against some of the Gulf States, and bombs were detonated in Bahrain and Kuwait. In 1987, Bahrain provided vital facilities for U.S. naval forces, which had been sent to the gulf to protect Kuwaiti oil tankers from attack by Iranian ships.

Bahrain remained a key American ally during the 1991 Gulf War, supporting naval vessels of the international coalition that liberated Kuwait after it had been invaded by Iraq in the summer of 1990. In 1991 and 1994, Bahrain solidified its security arrangements with the United States, thereby confirming its role as an important support base in the region.

A NEW CONSTITUTION

On March 6, 1999, Isa bin Salman al-Khalifa died of a heart attack at the age of 65. His son, Hamad bin Isa al-Khalifa, ascended to the throne.

To show Bahrain's desire to keep up with the Western world, the new emir decided to reform his country's government. He commissioned the drafting of a new national charter, pardoned hundreds of political prisoners (mostly Shiites), and granted women the right to vote. In February 2001, the government held a referendum on the charter, which would transform Bahrain into a constitutional monarchy governed by a king and a new, **bicameral** legislative body. Almost 90 percent of eligible voters cast their ballots, and the charter was overwhelmingly approved. The country's amended constitution subsequently went into effect in February 2002.

Elections for the 40 seats in the Chamber of Deputies, the elected house of the legislature, were held in October 2002. About 53 percent of Bahrain's population participated, despite a movement by some Shiites to boycott the election because the Chamber of Deputies would have the same powers as a Shura, or Consultative Council, appointed by the emir. Secular candidates won a slight majority with 21 seats, compared to 19 won by Islamist candidates. The next month, King Hamad appointed the 40 members of the Consultative Council. Among his appointments were a number of women and a Jewish man.

Bahrain's new National Assembly held its first meeting in December 2002, with the world watching to see if the small country's experiment with limited democracy would succeed.

The Grand Mosque is located in Manama; the al-Fateh Islamic Centre is nearby. About 85 percent of Bahrain's population follows Islam; most are Shiite Muslims.

Religion Politics and the Economy

The people of Bahrain pride themselves on the fact that their ancestors were among the first people to accept Islam, a religion that emerged from the Arabian desert in the 7th century A.D. Today, 85 percent of the people of Bahrain are Muslims. Most follow the Shiite branch of the faith, while a smaller number, which also includes the ruling Al Khalifa family, are Sunni Muslims. Shiites and Sunnis often live in separate communities and worship at different mosques.

Islam shares several characteristics with two other religions, Judaism and Christianity—most importantly, the idea of monotheism, or belief in a single God. The word "Islam" comes from the Arabic verb *aslama*, which means "to submit." The basis of the religion is submission to the will of Allah. It is based on the teachings of Muhammad, who dictated Allah's revelations in the Qur'an (or Koran), the Islamic holy book. The Qur'an and other Islamic writings teach Muslims how they are supposed to conduct their daily lives.

Islam is based on five basic precepts (sometimes called the pillars of Islam): *shahadah*, a profession of faith that there is no god but Allah, and that Muhammad was the messenger of Allah; *salat*, a prayer performed five times a day, always facing the holy city of Mecca; *zakat*, a charitable donation to people who are less fortunate; *sawm*, the practice of fasting from dawn to dusk during the month of Ramadan (the ninth month of the Hijri, or Islamic calendar, which is based on the lunar cycle); and *hajj*, a **pilgrimage** to Mecca that Muslims are encouraged to make during their lifetimes.

Although Islam is the official religion of the state, there are a small number of people who follow other religions—about 15 percent of the total population. These include Christians, Jews, Hindus, and Parsees (followers of an ancient Persian religion).

Men play a game of dominoes after breaking their fast during Ramadan, the ninth month of the Islamic calendar. During the daylight hours, Muslims are not permitted to eat or drink; after the sun has gone down, families eat a meal together and spend time relaxing.

POLITICAL AND RELIGIOUS TENSIONS

During the second half of the 20th century, Bahrain experienced a great deal of political tension. Some of this has been related to civil or labor issues. Economic problems during the 1950s and early 1960s eventually led to widespread labor protests in Bahrain, beginning with a strike against the Bahrain Petroleum Company on March 9, 1965. The government used the police and military to suppress labor protests and end the strike.

Over the next seven years, more protests—fueled by trade union leaders and militant Shiite Muslims—led to strikes and upheaval in Bahrain's electrical, aviation, aluminum, cable, and health care industries. The demands of workers were the same: an end to lay-offs, a right to unionize, improved safety procedures, and higher wages. In all instances, the government continued to use force to suppress these workers' movements. Although occasional worker strikes still take place in Bahrain, the incidence of labor protests has greatly diminished since the 1970s, as they have proven to be futile in bringing about change.

The split between Sunni and Shiite Muslims has frequently led to unrest, as Shiites have sought greater representation in Bahrain's political and economic affairs. Political events occurring outside of the country have also affected Bahrain. For example, the Ayatollah Khomeini's 1979 Islamic revolution in nearby Iran, where 90 percent of the population follows Shia Islam, led to Shiite protests in Bahrain, as well as several unsuccessful attempts to overthrow the Al Khalifa government.

Political unrest among Bahrain's Shiites continued in the 1990s, and the government's responses have often drawn international criticism. In 1994, Shiites calling for the restoration of the National Assembly, which had been dissolved nearly 20 years earlier, held protests that led to clashes with police. After several months of

A conservative Bahraini woman casts her vote at a polling station in Riffa during the October 2002 legislative election. Under Bahrain's 2002 charter, women are permitted to vote and to stand as candidates for election.

protests, the emir began negotiations with the Shiite leaders, but the talks ended by mid-1995. When bombs exploded at two large hotels in 1995 and 1996, the government and the media in Bahrain accused Iran of inciting violence among Bahrain's Shiite population—an allegation that Iran denied.

The Sunni-Shiite cleavage in Bahrain has had a significant effect on events in the country to this day and in all realms: political, economic, and religious. Given that the ruling family is Sunni and the majority of Bahrain's population is Shiite, and that the current leader of Bahrain proclaims that he wants democracy for his country, the problems between Sunnis and Shiites must be resolved.

THE GOVERNMENT OF BAHRAIN

Under the 2002 constitution, Bahrain is a constitutional monarchy, ruled by a king (prior to 2002, the Al Khalifa ruler was known as an emir). The constitution states that the succession of the office of king automatically passes from the ruler to his eldest son, unless a ruler specifies another member of the Al Khalifa family to succeed him.

It is common for the eldest son to serve an apprenticeship of sorts, serving as a deputy or in some sort of authority position until it is time for him to take control of the nation. It is also common for other Al Khalifa family members to occupy important positions in the government, serving as prime minister (Khalifa bin Salman al-Khalifa has held this position since 1971) or in the Council of Ministers, which oversees various government departments.

The constitution also provides for a bicameral legislature, the National Assembly. The two houses of the National Assembly are the Consultative Council, whose 40 members are appointed by the king; and the Chamber of Deputies, whose 40 members are elected by direct popular vote by citizens 20 years of age or older. Both appointed and elected legislators serve four-year terms. All legislation approved by the National Assembly must be ratified by the king in order to become law.

Bahrain has an independent legal and judicial system. The legal system draws upon Islamic religious law (*Sharia*); however, laws are also based on tribal law, English common law, and other legal sources. All residents are subject to the ***jurisdiction*** of Bahraini courts, which guarantee equality to all before the law (just as courts in the United States do).

The court system consists of *Sharia* courts and civil courts. *Sharia* courts rule on such personal cases as marriages, divorces, and inheritances, while criminal matters and other issues that affect the state are heard in the civil courts. Those who are unhappy with the ruling in either the civil or *Sharia* court may appeal the decisions to an appellate court. The country's highest court is the Supreme Court of Appeal.

The 2002 constitution established the Higher Judicial Council, which supervises the operation of the court system. The king heads the council and appoints judges proposed by the council.

Bahrain is divided into 12 municipalities, administered from Manama, the capital city, by a central municipal council, whose members are also appointed by the king. As a result, the central government has a great deal of control over local governmental affairs. The local governments are responsible for such things as sanitation, roads, police and emergency services, street lighting, public health, land reclamation, and providing clean water.

Political parties are technically not allowed, although informal political groups developed in 1973 when the country's first National Assembly was elected. The king has said he would favor the creation of political parties if doing so would not disrupt social unity.

The Bahraini Defense Force (BDF) numbered 11,000 in 2001. The BDF consists of an 8,500-member army, a 1,500-member air force, and a 1,000-member navy. Foreign personnel, chiefly Americans and Britains, contract with the BDF to supply support services. Bahrain's navy receives assistance (in the form of the loan of a *frigate* and training for its sailors) from the U.S. Navy, whose Fifth Fleet uses Bahrain's harbor facilities. Bahrain also has a coast guard, separate from the BDF, in which about 1,000 sailors are enlisted.

Military service is voluntary. However, native Bahraini Shiites are generally not accepted into the armed forces because the Sunni ruling establishment does not trust the Shiites, and does not want to give *dissidents* military training or allow them to gain positions in which they might have access to sensitive materials.

THE ECONOMY OF BAHRAIN

Over the years, Bahrain's economy has changed greatly. Until the early 20th century, pearling was Bahrain's principal source of income. The country's pearling fleet included thousands of ships and small boats, and close to half of the male population of Bahrain was engaged in harvesting or selling pearls. Indeed, pearls have special symbolic significance to the people of Bahrain.

At its height, as many as 5,000 small boats sailed from Bahrain to gather pearls during the three- to four-month season. Each boat carried from 6 to 15 men, and the equipment they used was simple. Lacking the modern scuba and snorkeling equipment we have today, the pearl divers used bone or tortoiseshell nose clips, leather thimbles to protect their fingers from the sharp coral, and wads of beeswax to put in each ear.

Divers often worked in very deep water, as the best pearl oysters

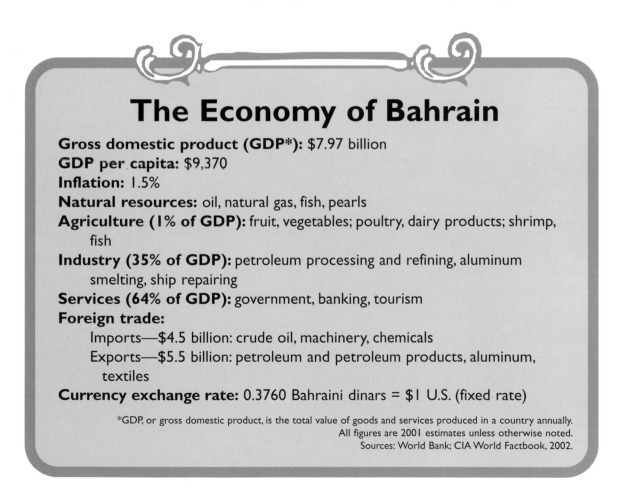

The Economy of Bahrain

Gross domestic product (GDP*): $7.97 billion
GDP per capita: $9,370
Inflation: 1.5%
Natural resources: oil, natural gas, fish, pearls
Agriculture (1% of GDP): fruit, vegetables; poultry, dairy products; shrimp, fish
Industry (35% of GDP): petroleum processing and refining, aluminum smelting, ship repairing
Services (64% of GDP): government, banking, tourism
Foreign trade:
    Imports—$4.5 billion: crude oil, machinery, chemicals
    Exports—$5.5 billion: petroleum and petroleum products, aluminum, textiles
Currency exchange rate: 0.3760 Bahraini dinars = $1 U.S. (fixed rate)

*GDP, or gross domestic product, is the total value of goods and services produced in a country annually.
All figures are 2001 estimates unless otherwise noted.
Sources: World Bank; CIA World Factbook, 2002.

were usually found at depths of 5 to 20 fathoms (a fathom is equal to six feet). They carried baskets with them to haul up their catch and had a lifeline attached to their wrists. When a diver was ready to come up, or if danger threatened, he tugged on the line and people at the surface hauled him up through the water to the boat.

After the pearls were brought to shore, they were carefully sorted according to size and color. Black pearls were considered bad luck, but brought huge prices from buyers around the world. The crew shared the profits from the sale of each catch.

The worldwide economic depression that began in the late 1920s severely hurt the pearl business, and the introduction of cultured pearls (that is, pearls that are cultivated or farmed) in the early 1930s effectively ended it. However, the pearling industry has not entirely disappeared from Bahrain, and festivals and songs remind people of these past "good old days." Pearls collected from Bahrain's waters are still a valuable collector's item. Some wealthy Bahrainis carry strings of pearls and use them to count off verses of the Qur'an when praying.

Bahraini sailors searching for pearls traditionally painted the upper hulls of their boats with shark oil, which smelled terrible but kept the wooden decks from cracking in the intense heat. They painted the section of the hull that sat underwater with a mixture of lime and sheep fat, which was supposed to discourage the growth of barnacles.

Fortunately for Bahrain, the decline in the demand for pearls coincided with a rise in the demand for oil. In 1925, Sheikh Isa bin al-Khalifa gave a company from the United States permission to explore for oil in Bahrain. Soon, large quantities of the valuable resource were discovered. In 1932, Bahrain became the first country in the Arabian Gulf region to export oil.

Today, Bahrain's oil production is minimal by the standards of other Gulf nations. The United Arab Emirates, for instance, produces about 2 million barrels a day, while Bahrain's daily production is less than 50,000 barrels. Bahrain does, however, refine a large quantity of oil from Saudi Arabia, which arrives in the country through an undersea pipeline.

Since the 1930s, oil production and refining have dominated Bahrain's economy. However, the country cannot be dependent on oil alone. This has prompted efforts to diversify and develop other industries. By the early 1960s, Bahrain had expanded its oil industry into petroleum refining, petrochemical processing, manufacturing, ship repair, and services in the industrial, financial, and business sectors. The aim was twofold: to accelerate economic growth and to provide employment for the people of Bahrain.

In the 1970s, the government established Aluminum Bahrain

Tanks at an oil refinery in Bahrain. Bahrain was the first country in the Gulf region to export oil; however, it has much smaller reserves of this resource than other Arab countries like Saudi Arabia or Kuwait.

(ALBA) as a joint venture with Saudi Arabia. Aluminum **smelting** remains an important industry in Bahrain, and ALBA is the one of the world's three largest producers of aluminum and aluminum alloys.

Another offshoot of the oil industry is Bahrain's natural gas production facilities. Natural gas occurs underground in combination with crude oil. For a long time, the gas was released through the oil wells and escaped into the air. In 1979, the government of Bahrain established a company to collect and process the natural gas into propane, butane, and naphtha.

The government controls the oil and gas industry, most heavy manufacturing, and the bulk of the transportation and communications sectors. However, it has undertaken efforts to privatize the economy. Today private companies own banks, light manufacturing plants, and other businesses.

Banking and financial services are businesses that Bahrain entered in the late 1970s. Lebanon, a small Arab country on the coast of the Mediterranean Sea, was the banking center of the Middle East until 1975, when a civil war between the country's Christian and Muslim populations began. The 15-year-long war devastated Lebanon, making it one of the world's most dangerous places. Bahrain's government capitalized on Lebanon's misfortune by making a concerted effort to attract banks that had been based in Beirut to move to Manama, Bahrain's capital. These efforts paid off as Bahrain established itself as an important financial center by the mid-1980s.

The government has also made huge efforts to promote tourism. Today, some 2.5 million people visit Bahrain each year, and tourism accounts for 11 percent of the nation's annual gross domestic product (GDP).

Agriculture is also an important part of Bahrain's economy. Like its Arabian Gulf neighbors, Bahrain has aimed for agricultural self-sufficiency, and farms in the country produce about 75 percent of the fruits and vegetables that Bahrain's population consumes. The main crops are dates, tomatoes, onions, and melons. The country also produces a large portion of its milk, poultry, and egg requirements.

The Gulf War (1990–91) was both a blessing and a curse for Bahrain. On one hand, business

The Bahraini dinar is divided into 1,000 fils. Notes are available in the following denominations: 500 fils (brown), one dinar (red), five dinars (blue), 10 dinars (green), and 20 dinars (peach). Coins come in units of 10, 25, 50, and 100 fils.

was great. Foreign sailors, soldiers, and journalists filled the country's hotels and restaurants, spending their money there. And entrepreneurs flocked to the region as well, hoping to cash in on a post-war rebuilding boom in Kuwait. However, in the long run Bahrain found its financial-services industry damaged by the war, which, along with a ***recession*** that hit in the early 1990s, left the country's economy in a weakened state.

To encourage private-sector investment, the government instituted an innovative series of industrial development and employment initiatives. These initiatives were further strengthened and enhanced by legislation allowing 100 percent foreign ownership to onshore companies (previously, a citizen or company of Bahrain had to own a percentage of any private company that wanted to operated in the country), and other changes. The government has also maintained its commitment to zero taxes on corporate and personal income. Furthermore, there is low inflation and no restriction on the movement of funds.

International law firms, insurance companies, certified public accountants, management and public-relations consultants, financial analysts, and advisers are all represented in the well-integrated services sector of Bahrain. This has, of course, stimulated the growth of other related financial establishments, including the Bahrain Stock Market, the money-exchange sector, the real estate and construction businesses, and other commercial enterprises.

The Bahrain Monetary Agency (BMA), a supervisory agency, is the force behind the program designed to improve the already high reputation of Bahrain in banking circles. The BMA maintains solid reporting and accounting regulations, which strictly adhere to international practices. It conforms to international standards in the area of supervision, and focuses increasingly on the quality rather than the quantity of bank assets. Under the BMA's Deposit Protection program, the commercial bank deposits of both residents and non-residents, in local or foreign currency, are protected up to a prescribed level in the event of the liquidation of a bank operating in Bahrain. This is similar to the FDIC laws in place in the United States, which insure the money people put into banks to make certain they will have access to their funds if there is a a problem with the bank. Bahrain has consistently been ranked third in the world (after

An investor speaks on the phone while conducting business at Bahrain's stock exchange in Manama. Bahrain has become an important financial center in the Middle East.

Early flags of Bahrain were red, representing the color of the Kharidjite Muslims. In 1820, after a treaty was signed with Great Britain, a vertical white stripe was added to symbolize the truce. In 1933, to distinguish the flag from similar flags of the Gulf region, the stripe became an eight-pointed white pattern.

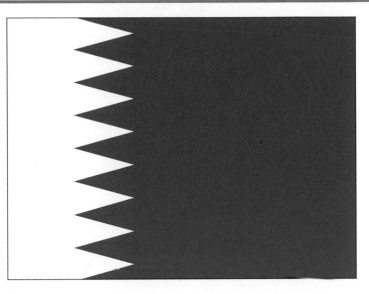

Hong Kong and Singapore) on the American Heritage Foundation's Index of Economic Freedom.

The population of Bahrain is small, and foreigners hold many jobs. Even though Bahrain is one of the few countries in the Gulf region with more native citizens than foreign workers (there are three Bahraini citizens for every two non-Bahrainis), there are a large number of foreigners in the work force.

Foreign workers, both skilled and unskilled, first were drawn to Bahrain in the 1930s, when oil was first discovered. Today, most manual laborers in Bahrain are from underdeveloped countries such as Thailand, India, Sri Lanka, the Philippines, and a variety of countries on the African continent. Skilled workers, such as engineers, come from Europe and other Arab nations. Most foreign workers are hired on a temporary basis, and cannot purchase real estate in Bahrain or apply for citizenship.

Bahrain's currency is the Bahraini dinar, which is tied to the value of the U.S. dollar. In rural areas, many transactions are made by bartering and trade rather than with dinars.

A farmer picks the fruits from a date palm during the harvest. There are many small farms on Bahrain, and unlike some of its Gulf neighbors the country produces much of its own food.

The People

Bahrain has been among the more sophisticated of the Arab countries because for thousands of years merchants, sailors, and traders have brought the islands into contact with people from distant places. In many ways, Bahrain's society is relatively open and liberal, welcoming what foreign visitors have to offer. Merchants have long been the dominant class, establishing a business-oriented culture that values the accumulation of wealth. At the same time, Bahraini society continues to be shaped by conservative Islamic values, especially those of the rural Shiite population.

Most of Bahrain's citizens are devout Muslims and live their lives according to the rules laid down in the Qur'an. Yet compared to their Arab neighbors, Bahrainis have an accepting attitude toward non-Muslims. The minority practicing such faiths as Judaism, Christianity, Bahai, Hindu, and Parsee are generally not persecuted for their beliefs.

FAMILY LIFE

As in many Arab countries, the typical Bahraini family consists of at least three generations under one roof: father, mother, unmarried children, their married sons with their wives and children, and a divorced or widowed daughter, sister, or mother. Daughters leave their parents' home when they are married, going to live in the home of their husbands' fathers.

The family is considered to be the foundation of life in Bahrain, and can be an important part of any person's social or legal identity. Children learn about this concept at an early age. They are taught to have respect for elders and to behave in ways that protect the honor of their family. Behavior that is even slightly rebellious or improper threatens the honor of the family.

A woman wears a traditional costume—robe and headdress—at the Heritage Center in Bahrain.

In the Arab world, it has been a tradition that women remain at home while men worked. Today, however, women are playing an increasingly important role in the business and professional life of Bahrain. Government regulations ensure that women have the right to work, and women are permitted to vote in national elections and run for public office. When the country became independent in 1971, just 5 percent of women worked; by 2002 that figure was nearly 40 percent

Most of Bahrain's population is clustered in the northern part of the country, around the capital city, Manama, and on Muharraq Island.

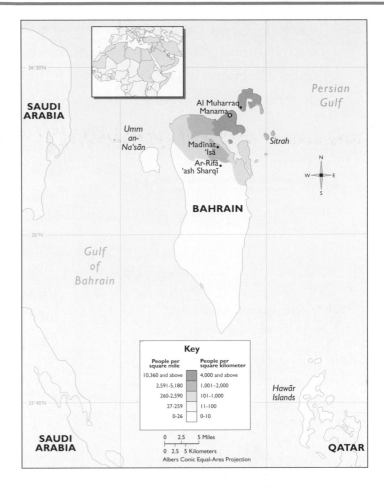

and climbing. Today more Bahraini women hold university degrees than men.

Although when compared to the other Arab nations, Bahrain is liberal in its dress, by the standards of the West, it is quite conservative. There are ***taboos*** against any unnecessary exposure of the body—by men or women. Visitors to the country are expected to respect these traditions and dress modestly. In the cities, some people wear Western-style clothing. However, traditional dress remains predominant in many areas.

For men, this includes a loose cotton garment called a *thobe*, which has long white sleeves and no collar, but often has a tassel attached to the neck opening. When the weather turns cool, the *thobe* is often covered with a woolen robe called a *bisht*. Men also wear a head cloth (*ghura*), which in contrast to the white robe is often checkered. The head cloth is held in place by a twisted black or white cord (called an *agal*).

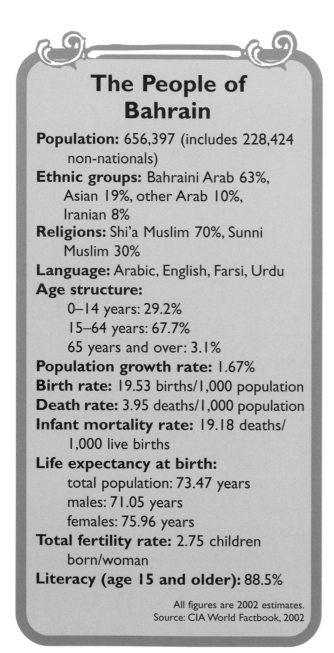

The People of Bahrain

Population: 656,397 (includes 228,424 non-nationals)

Ethnic groups: Bahraini Arab 63%, Asian 19%, other Arab 10%, Iranian 8%

Religions: Shi'a Muslim 70%, Sunni Muslim 30%

Language: Arabic, English, Farsi, Urdu

Age structure:
0–14 years: 29.2%
15–64 years: 67.7%
65 years and over: 3.1%

Population growth rate: 1.67%

Birth rate: 19.53 births/1,000 population

Death rate: 3.95 deaths/1,000 population

Infant mortality rate: 19.18 deaths/ 1,000 live births

Life expectancy at birth:
total population: 73.47 years
males: 71.05 years
females: 75.96 years

Total fertility rate: 2.75 children born/woman

Literacy (age 15 and older): 88.5%

All figures are 2002 estimates.
Source: CIA World Factbook, 2002

Although regulations on women's clothing in Bahrain are not as strict as in other Islamic countries, such as Saudi Arabia, most women wear the *abayah*, a large cloak that covers them from head to foot. Beneath the dark *abayah*, women might wear colorful clothing. Some women wear veils, although this is not required.

Children might wear both traditional clothing or Western-style t-shirts and blue jeans. At some schools, the students are required to wear uniforms similar to those worn at private schools in the United States.

Most houses in Bahrain appear similar, and are built of bricks made from cement and lime. There are few wooden structures, as wood for construction is not available on the islands. One of the more interesting features of older Bahraini homes is the wind tower. This structure, located on the top floor, was constructed with shafts so that any breezes are funneled into the lower floors of the house. To facilitate this, houses in Bahrain were usually built several stories tall. The higher a house is, the better the opportunity to catch the desert breezes. Lower rooms often have small windows that are covered with shutters, but upper stories have large,

Many Bahraini families go camping in the desert. This is both a reminder of their heritage as a desert people and an opportunity to retreat from the hustle and bustle of city life.

arched windows to help with ventilation. Today, of course, modern air conditioning systems helps keep things cool in most homes.

One of the most prized possessions of a Bahraini home are its rugs. These could range from elaborate Oriental-style rugs to hand-woven, but still beautiful, rugs that have been locally made. Interestingly enough, rugs are so important that they almost serve as a form of currency. Families pass them down from one generation to the next, and wealthy businessmen often invest in antique rugs as a form of insurance against inflation or hard economic times.

TRADITIONAL MEALS

A typical Bahraini meal consists of a rice dish, accompanied with a flat bread, vegetables, and some kind of fish or meat—often lamb, chicken, or beef. A traditional dish is ghouzi, a whole roasted lamb stuffed with chicken, rice, and eggs. Muslims are not supposed to eat pork or drink alcohol.

Meals are traditionally served on a carpeted floor, and food is eaten with the right hand, even if a person is left-handed. In fact, it is considered extremely rude to offer something to another person with the left hand, or to accept something using that hand. If it is absolutely impossible for a person to avoid using his or her left

Men drink coffee together in the Gulf Hotel, Manama. In Arab countries, certain traditions are observed when it comes to drinking coffee (*ghawah*).

hand, they might first use the expression *Shimaalin ma tishnaak*, which means, "The left does not injure you." The appropriate reply is *Shimaalak yamiin*, meaning, "your left is right."

An important part of eating a traditional meal in Bahrain is the coffee that is served both at the beginning and at the end of a meal. Arabic coffee, or *ghawah*, is unsweetened, but may be flavored with cardamom or cloves. The coffee is served in small cups that do not have handles. The cups are only filled halfway, and a polite guest never accepts more than three cups. Once the third cup is finished, it is considered polite for a guest to hold out the empty cup and tilt it from side to side. This is an indication that the cup should be taken away.

After the coffee has been finished at the end of a meal, it is time for guests to leave. Relaxed conversation is common before a meal, but guests do not continue to make small talk afterward.

IMPORTANT RITUALS

Three events are common in everyone's life: birth, marriage, and death. The people of Bahrain celebrate or observe each of these important events in unique ways.

Prior to giving birth, a Bahraini woman returns to her father's house, where special herbs and food are prepared for her. She drinks a customary cup of water and eats three dates. Once the baby is born, it is rubbed with herbs, wrapped in a soft cotton cloth, and placed in its cradle. To introduce it to Islam, the call to prayer is recited in the baby's right ear and a prayer is recited in the baby's left ear. In Bahrain, infants are usually named on the second day following their birth. Names are often those of other family members. For example, a baby boy might be given the name of his grandfather, or of another significant male in the family's history.

Despite Bahrain's relative modernity, marriages are usually not left to chance or love. It might surprise some Westerners to learn that marriages are, for the most part, still arranged here by the parents of the prospective bride and groom. The ideal match is considered to be between a man and his father's brother's daughter, or between a woman and her father's brother's son. These are known as patrilateral parallel cousins. This is done to ensure that property and rank remains within a single line of male descent.

A groom must pay a dowry, usually a combination of money, furniture, and even real estate, to the bride's family. This is different from other cultures in which the bride is expected to pay the dowry. The value of the dowry is often quite high; it is kept in the bride's name so that it the couple should ever divorce, she will be able to support herself.

Three Bahrainis who have just finished a prayer session walk from their mosque past a McDonald's restaurant. Although Bahrain's is an Arab culture, Western influences are apparent throughout the country.

A few days before a wedding, a good luck party is held for the bride. Only females are invited to this party. The bride sits in a chair with a basket of sweets, while the other women recite religious verses. After this four women hold a green cloth over the bride's head and lift it up and down while the others sing. This is supposed to bring the bride luck in her marriage. The night before a wedding, intricate patterns are painted on the bride's hands and feet with henna, a reddish-brown dye. It is customary that the bride does not have to do any work in her new house until the patterns have faded away.

Social custom in Bahrain, as in all parts of the Islamic world, puts a great premium on the respect due to elders. Parents and grandparents in particular are respected and held in great esteem by their children, who are expected to care for them as they grow older. The oldest male in a Bahraini family has the most authority and is considered the primary decision-maker. The oldest woman's authority extends only as far as her influence over her husband or, if she is a widow, over her eldest son.

When a person dies, he or she is usually buried before sunset of the next day, in accordance with the laws of the Qur'an. The body is wrapped in a sheet and buried in a grave with only a simple marker. No matter how wealthy someone may have been in life, in death everyone is buried in the same way—simply and without ornamentation. This is because it is assumed that the deceased person is now in paradise and needs no elaborate reminders of his or her time on earth.

EDUCATION AND HEALTH CARE

Bahrain has one of the highest ***literacy*** rates in the Arab world, thanks to strong government support for education. According to 2002 estimates, more than 88 percent of Bahrainis over the age of 15 can read and write (about 92 percent of men and 84 percent of women).

Bahrain established the first public education system in the Arabian Gulf region in 1919. In 1975, new laws regarding education were passed; these extended the time required to complete high school from two to three years.

Today, public education is free to all, and is required by law for all boys and girls between the ages of 6 and 15. In addition, there are private religious schools throughout the nation. Bahraini laws provide structure for private education, outlining guidelines for curriculum content as well as for staffing levels and administrative organization.

Bahrainis who complete high school can continue their studies at several colleges, including the University of Bahrain, which was established in 1986 in Manama. The university has bachelor's and graduate degree programs in such fields as education, civil engineering, and business administration. For professionals already in the workplace, the university offers continuing-education programs.

Another institution of higher education in Manama is the College of Health Sciences, founded in 1976, which trains physicians, nurses, and other health professionals.

Health services in Bahrain are free for all citizens. The country has a health-care network that includes more than 20 health centers and clinics, five maternity hospitals, a psychiatric hospital, a hospital for elderly patients, and the Salmaniya Medical Complex. Nearly 7,000 people are employed by the country's Ministry of Health.

TRANSPORTATION

Bahrain is a major air transportation hub for the Middle East region, and together with the governments of Qatar, Oman, and Abu Dhabi (part of the UAE), it operates an international airline called Gulf Air. The airport at Muharraq Island is a large international facility.

A well-developed road network, consisting of approximately 1,966 miles (3,164 km) of roads, links the country's population centers. Causeways link the island of Bahrain to Muharraq and Sitrah islands. The King Fahd Causeway, opened in 1986, links Bahrain to Saudi Arabia.

Mina Sulman serves as the major commercial port, while Sitrah Island contains the main oil port.

A national bus company operates throughout the country. There are

> Calligraphy—the art of producing artistic, stylized, or elegant handwriting—is central to Muslim culture and is especially honored for its connection to religious life.

no railroads. Many Bahrainis rely largely on walking to get around, especially in rural areas, although the heat of summer limits physical activity.

ARTS AND CULTURE

Bahrain has become known as an extensive entertainment center, with concerts, sporting contests, and cultural events. Events include performances by Western pop-music acts, traveling ballet and opera troupes, Arab musical stars, plays performed by international actors, and exhibition sports matches. Bahrain

A woman shops for food at a grocery store in Bahrain.

offers facilities such as a 4,000-seat indoor theater, as well as conference centers, major outdoor arenas, and well-known hotels. The modern forms of entertainment found in Manama, such as movies, are aimed primarily at foreigners.

Bahrain has an extensive and sophisticated communications network, including two AM radio stations, three FM stations, and two television stations. There are two daily newspapers in Arabic and one in English, seven weekly publications covering various subject areas, and a number of other magazines. While Bahrain is liberal and open for the most part, the government does exercise **censorship** over reports and commentary on domestic affairs. Bahrainis generally stay well informed about international events through foreign publications and satellite television links. In 1995, Bahrain gained access to the Internet, linking this nation with the global community in yet another way.

Traditional Bahraini culture reflects its Islamic, mercantile, and tribal roots. Graceful dhows—Arab boats used for fishing and pearling—exhibit a high degree of craftsmanship, as do traditional jewelry and the elegantly designed homes of rulers and merchants. Traditional performing arts include ceremonial dances accompanied by drums, readings of the Qur'an, and storytelling. Bahraini poets carry on established traditions while also exploring new themes. The Bahrain National Museum, which opened in 1988 in Manama, features exhibits of crafts, historical documents, and archaeological artifacts.

Other activities that Bahrainis enjoy include horse racing (great care is given to the breeding and raising of the Arabian horse) and falconry (the art of hunting with specially trained birds). These two activities are rooted in ancient Arab tradition; however, for the most part their practice is restricted to the wealthy. More accessible activities and sports include soccer, tennis, scuba diving, snorkeling, boating, fishing, and racing dune buggies. Parks and shops are also important, especially as places to keep cool in during the heat of the day.

Children's games are specific to boys and girls. Boys are encouraged to be outgoing and competitive. Games played by them include racing small boats and playing hide-and-seek. Girls are encouraged to play in the home or within the home's enclosed courtyard. They often play with dolls, or participate in games that imitate the activities of their mothers.

An old house on Muharraq Island. The large windows on the upper floors are intended to help ventilate the home. Most of Bahrain's people are located on the main island; Muharraq, the second-largest of the country's islands, is connected to Bahrain Island by a causeway.

Communities

ahrain offers a wealth of experiences for both native residents and visitors alike. Manama, the capital city, manages to combine both the old and the new. Located at the northeastern tip of Bahrain Island, Manama has been mentioned in Arabic writings nearly 700 years old.

Over the years Manama's population has grown steadily. About 67,000 people lived in the city when Bahrain became independent in 1971. Today, it is home to more than 150,000 people—about one-quarter of Bahrain's population.

One of the city's major attractions is the National Museum, which has excellent exhibits explained in both Arabic and English. The museum has artifacts and informative displays related to 7,000 years of Bahrain's history. Another interesting museum is the Bait al-Qur'an, the only museum in the world devoted to the holy book of Islam.

Manama's *souk*, or marketplace, is a popular spot where

the savvy shopper can find bargains on just about anything, from electronic items to clothing and jewelry. The entrance to the *souk* is guarded by the Bab al-Bahrain ("gateway to Bahrain"), a large white building.

Manama is home to the largest building in the country—the al-Fatih Mosque, which can hold up to 7,000 worshippers. The University of Bahrain, founded in 1986, is also located in Manama.

Not far from Manama are several interesting sites dating back to the Dilmun civilization. The remains of the Ad-Diraz Temple, including the stone base of what was probably an altar and the bases of many columns, are about 3 miles (5 km) west of the capital city. Barbar Temple includes three temples, built more than 4,000 years ago and dedicated to Enki, god of wisdom and water. It is located about 6 miles (10 km) outside of Manama. And an

The skyline of Manama, capital of Bahrain and the country's largest city.

ancient tomb complex is located near the village of A'ali.

Another site near Manama is Qal'at al-Bahrain, the country's main archaeological site. Excavations on this site, where a Portuguese fort once stood, began during the 1950s. Archaeologists soon found that the 15th-century fort had been built on top of the rubble of older cities. Seven layers of occupation have been found, the oldest dating back to 2800 B.C.

MUHARRAQ ISLAND

While Manama has been modernized in recent years, communities on Muharraq Island retain much of the flavor of an older Bahrain. According to Bahrain's 2001 census, 91,939 people live on Muharraq Island.

Among the interesting things to see on the island are two well-preserved traditional houses dating from the early 19th century, the Bait Shaikh Isa Bin and the Bait Seyadi. The former is of interest in part because it still has a working wind tower on its roof—a structure used in the days before air conditioning to direct cool breezes into a home's interior.

Two Portuguese forts dating from the 16th century are popular among visitors to Muharraq Island. The skyline of Manama is visible from Abu Mahir Fort. Arad Fort has been partially restored. Another popular sport for tourists is a small dhow building yard, where the traditional Bahraini fishing boats are constructed. And some people consider the island's *souk* to be even more interesting than the one in the capital.

Bahrain's international airport is located on Muharraq Island;

An elderly Bahraini man (right) serves traditional Arabic sweets to a customer, a day before the start of Eid al-Adha, a three-day feast that marks the end of the period of pilgrimage (*hajj*) to Mecca.

access to the airport from Manama is available through a causeway.

OTHER IMPORTANT COMMUNITIES

Riffa (population 79,985) is located about 12 miles (19 km) from Manama. A notable tourist spot is the Riffa Fort, built in 1812, which has been restored and is open for public tours.

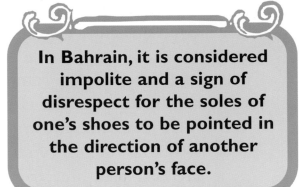

In Bahrain, it is considered impolite and a sign of disrespect for the soles of one's shoes to be pointed in the direction of another person's face.

Sitrah Island (pop. 43,910) is an important industrial area, which contains petrochemical processing plants and an oil storage depot. The island is connected by causeway to Manama.

Since Bahrain became independent in 1971, its government has built several modern towns for its people. The first of these was Isa Town, which was built in the 1970s and is now home to some 36,833 people. Isa Town is known as a place with nice homes, good shopping, and excellent government-run schools. After Isa Town was completed, the government began work on Hamad Town in 1982. The community was incorporated two years later. Today, Hamad Town is home to about 52,718 people.

FESTIVALS AND CELEBRATIONS

In the past, the people of Bahrain celebrated various festivals related to underground fresh water and the seasonal return of the pearl-fishing boats. However, these festivals are no longer held since the pearling industry has died out and desalinated water has replaced the underground aquifers.

The most popular holidays are those related to Islam, such as Eid al-Fitr, Eid al-Adha, and Ashura. Secular holidays include Labour Day (May 1), and Bahrain's national holiday (December 16).

Ramadan, the ninth month of the Islamic lunar calendar, is the holy month of fasting. Adult Muslims are expected to abstain from eating, drinking, and other activites between sunup and sundown. After night falls, families gather to eat together.

Eid al-Fitr (the feast of fast-breaking) is a festival marking the end of Ramadan. It begins with the sighting of the new moon on the first day of Shawwal, the tenth month in the Islamic calendar, and generally lasts for three days. Muslims take part in communal prayers, either in a mosque or an open space outside the city, and everyone must offer charity to the poor. Friends, relatives, and neighbors meet in mosques and on streets, or visit one another, exchanging congratulations and small gifts.

Eid al-Adha (the Festival of the Sacrifice) takes place on the tenth day of the Islamic month, known as Dhul-Hijjah, This is the last month of the Islamic calendar. Eid al-Adha marks the end of the annual Hajj period, during which millions of Muslims from around the world make their pilgrimage to Mecca.

The festival also commemorates an important moment in ancient history—the willingness of the patriarch Abraham to sacrifice his son in response to a command from God. According to the Muslim account of the events, Allah was satisfied with Abraham's willingness to slaughter his son Ishmael, and told Abraham to sacrifice a sheep instead. Traditionally, Muslims throughout the world slaughter a sheep in observance of this festival. One-third of the meat is to be distributed to the poor, one-third given to neighbors and relatives, and one-third eaten by the Muslim's immediate family.

Bahrain's large Shiite community also celebrates Ashura, a religious festival that marks the death of Hussein, the grandson of the Prophet Muhammad, at the battle of Karbala, near Babylon, in A.D. 680. Shiites believe that Hussein was the rightful Islamic caliph, who tried to protect Muhammad's teachings from distortion; he was killed by the armies of the Umayyad caliph Yazid, a Sunni Muslim.

Ashura is the most important religious festival celebrated in Bahrain after Eid al-Fitr and Eid al-Adha. Processions throughout the city streets are led by men ***flagellating*** themselves to express their sorrow at Hussein's death.

In addition to these festivals, there are several one-day holidays that Bahrainis observe throughout the year. These include Muhammad's birthday and the date of his ascension into heaven. However, these are not marked by large-scale public celebrations as are the longer, more significant holidays.